מִגְדַּל בָּבֶל
The Tower of Babel

THE ISIDORE & FAY RUDIN
CHILDREN'S LITERATURE COLLECTION
established June, 1995
The Jewish Education Center of Cleveland

Funded by the Isidore & Fay Rudin Fund of
The Jewish Community Federation of Cleveland

מִגְדַּל בָּבֶל
The Tower of Babel

Adapted by
Alison Greengard

Illustrated by
Carol Racklin-Siegel

EXCERPTED FROM
THE BOOK OF GENESIS

EKS Publishing Co., Albany, California

Adapted by
Alison Greengard

Illustrated by
Carol Racklin-Siegel

Editor
Jessica Goldstein

Book Design
Irene Imfeld

The Tower of Babel © 2001 by EKS Publishing Co. Printed in Canada. No part of this book may be transmitted or reproduced by any means, electronic or mechanical, without written permission, except for brief quotations included in critical articles and reviews. For information contact the publisher.

EKS Publishing Co.
P.O. Box 9750, Berkeley, CA 94709-0750
e-mail: orders@ekspublishing.com
Phone (510) 558-9200 Fax (510) 558-9255
www.ekspublishing.com

First Printing, July 2001
ISBN 0-939144-35-2

To my husband Tom
for twenty-five years of
love and support.
—Alison

To my children, Rachel, Jackie and
Daniel Siegel, who I learn
from every day.
—Carol

Introduction

The *Tower of Babel* is the second volume in the EKS Publishing series of Bible stories for young readers. The story of *The Tower of Babel* appears in the eleventh chapter of Genesis, and we have not changed the Hebrew text in this book. Each page offers a meaningful—but not always literal—translation. For readers studying Hebrew, we have included a literal translation at the end of the story. A glossary at the back of the book gives the meaning and pronunciation of each word in *The Tower of Babel*. The glossary lists words exactly as they appear in the story.

The Tower of Babel tells a small but powerful story. Though it occupies only nine verses in the Bible, the story of Babel describes nothing less profound than the development of distinct human cultures: how people who shared a language and city came to be dispersed throughout the world with separate languages and cultures. The Hebrew in the story plays on the similarity between the words בָּבֶל (Babel, the location of the tower) and בָּלַל (confuse, what God did to the world's single language). The text associates excessive human ambition with sin, and biblical authors were likely trying to associate the Babel in this story with Babylonia, a civilization famous for ziggurats that stretched high into the heavens. In fact, rabbis of the Midrash claim that the Babylonian king Nimrod oversaw construction of the tower in this story.

We hope that readers of all ages will enjoy this telling of *The Tower of Babel* and come to appreciate the language and beauty of the Hebrew Bible.

וַיְהִי כָל הָאָרֶץ שָׂפָה אֶחָת וּדְבָרִים אֲחָדִים.
וַיְהִי בְּנָסְעָם מִקֶּדֶם וַיִּמְצְאוּ בִקְעָה
בְּאֶרֶץ שִׁנְעָר וַיֵּשְׁבוּ שָׁם.

Long ago, people in the world spoke just one language. They traveled from the East until they came to a valley in the land of Shinar and settled there.

וַיֹּאמְרוּ אִישׁ אֶל רֵעֵהוּ הָבָה נִלְבְּנָה לְבֵנִים וְנִשְׂרְפָה לִשְׂרֵפָה וַתְּהִי לָהֶם הַלְּבֵנָה לְאָבֶן וְהַחֵמָר הָיָה לָהֶם לַחֹמֶר.

Everyone said to one another, "Let's make bricks and fire them." And so they had bricks to use for stones and tar for mortar.

וַיֹּאמְרוּ הָבָה נִבְנֶה לָּנוּ עִיר וּמִגְדָּל וְרֹאשׁוֹ בַשָּׁמַיִם וְנַעֲשֶׂה לָּנוּ שֵׁם פֶּן נָפוּץ עַל פְּנֵי כָל הָאָרֶץ.

They said, "Come, let's build ourselves a city and a tower whose top will reach the sky. We'll make a name for ourselves so we won't be scattered all over the world."

וַיֵּרֶד יְהֹוָה לִרְאֹת אֶת הָעִיר וְאֶת הַמִּגְדָּל אֲשֶׁר בָּנוּ בְּנֵי הָאָדָם. וַיֹּאמֶר יְהֹוָה הֵן עַם אֶחָד וְשָׂפָה אַחַת לְכֻלָּם וְזֶה הַחִלָּם לַעֲשׂוֹת וְעַתָּה לֹא יִבָּצֵר מֵהֶם כֹּל אֲשֶׁר יָזְמוּ לַעֲשׂוֹת.

God came down to see the city and the tower that the people had built.
God said, "They are one people with one language, and this is just the beginning of what they will do! Now nothing they want to do will be impossible!"

הָבָה נֵרְדָה וְנָבְלָה שָׁם שְׂפָתָם אֲשֶׁר לֹא יִשְׁמְעוּ אִישׁ שְׂפַת רֵעֵהוּ.

"Come, let us go down and mix up their language so they won't understand each other."

וַיָּפֶץ יְהוָה אֹתָם מִשָּׁם
עַל פְּנֵי כָל הָאָרֶץ
וַיַּחְדְּלוּ לִבְנֹת הָעִיר.

God scattered the people all over the world,
and they stopped building the city.

עַל כֵּן קָרָא שְׁמָהּ
בָּבֶל כִּי שָׁם בָּלַל
יְהוָה שְׂפַת כָּל הָאָרֶץ.

The city was named Babel,
because that is where God made
a babble out of the world's language.

Literal Translation

Now the earth had one language and few words. While they (people) were traveling from the east, they found a valley in the land of Shinar and settled there.

Each man said to the other, "Let's make bricks and we will burn them completely." And they had for themselves bricks for stone. And they had bitumen for mortar.

They said, "Let us build ourselves a city, and a tower whose top will be in the heavens. And we will make a name for ourselves, lest we be scattered on the face of the earth."

God descended to see the city and the tower that the sons of man (people) had built. And God said, "Look! They are one people with one language, and this is what they begin to do! Now nothing that they decide to do will be withheld from them! Come, let us go down there and confuse their language so that each person will not understand the speech of the other."

And God scattered them from there upon the face of the earth, and they stopped building the city. Therefore, it was called Babel, because it was there that God confused the language of the world.

Glossary

א

אֶחָד	e-**chad**	one
אֲחָדִים	a-cha-**dim**	few
אֶחָת	e-**chat**	one
אַחַת	a-**chat**	one
אִישׁ	eesh	man, each one
אֶל	el	to
אֲשֶׁר	a-**sher**	so that/that/which
אֵת	et	not translatable
אֹתָם	o-**tam**	them

ב

בְּאֶרֶץ	b-**e**-rets	in the land of
בָּבֶל	ba-**vel**	Babel
בָּלַל	ba-**lal**	he confused
בָּנוּ	ba-**nu**	they built
בְּנֵי	b-**nay**	the children of/the sons of
בְּנֵי הָאָדָם	b-**nay** ha-a-**dam**	the people
בְּנָסְעָם	b-nas-**am**	while traveling
בִּקְעָה	veek-**a**	valley
בַּשָּׁמַיִם	vash-sha-**ma**-yeem	in the heavens

ה

הָאָדָם	ha-a-**dam**	the human being/man
הָאָרֶץ	ha-**a**-rets	the earth
הָבָה	**ha**-va	let us
הַחִלָּם	ha-chil-**lam**	what they begin
הָיָה	ha-**ya**	was
הַלְּבֵנָה	hal-l-vay-**na**	brick
הַמִּגְדָּל	ham-mig-**dal**	the tower
הֵן	**hayn**	look!
הָעִיר	ha-**eer**	the city

ו

וְאֵת	v-**et**	not translatable
וּדְבָרִים	oo-d-va-**reem**	and words
וְהַחֵמָר	v-ha-chay-**mar**	the bitumen/tar
וְזֶה	v-**ze**	and this
וַיֹּאמֶר	vay-**yo**-mer	he said
וַיֹּאמְרוּ	vay-yo-m-**ru**	they said
וַיְהִי	vay-**hee**	and there was
וַיַּחְדְּלוּ	vay-yach-d-**loo**	they stopped
וַיִּמְצְאוּ	vay-yim-ts-**oo**	they found
וַיָּפֶץ	vay-ya-**fets**	he scattered

ו

וַיֵּרֶד	vay-**yay**-red	he came down
וַיֵּשְׁבוּ	vay-yay-sh-**voo**	and they settled
וּמִגְדָּל	oo-mig-**dal**	and the tower
וְנָבְלָה	v-na-v-**la**	and let us confuse
וְנַעֲשֶׂה	v-na-a-**se**	we will make
וְנִשְׂרְפָה לִשְׂרֵפָה	v-nis-r-**fa** lis-ray-**fa**	and let us fire them/ burn them completely
וְעַתָּה	v-at-**ta**	and now
וְרֹאשׁוֹ	v-ro-**sho**	and its top
וַתְּהִי	vat-t-**hee**	and it was

י

יִבָּצֵר	yeeb-ba-**tsayr**	will be witheld
יְהוָה	a-do-**nai**	God
יָזְמוּ	ya-z-**moo**	they begin
יִשְׁמְעוּ	yish-m-**oo**	they will understand
כִּי	**kee**	because/for
כָּל	**chol**	all
כֹּל	kol	all
כָּל הָאָרֶץ	kol ha-**a**-rets	all the earth
כָּל הָאָרֶץ	chol ha-**a**-rets	all the earth

ל

לֹא	lo	nothing, no, not
לְאָבֶן	l-**a**-ven	for stone
לְבֵנִים	l-vay-**neem**	for bricks
לִבְנֹת	leev-**not**	to build
לָהֶם	la-**hem**	for them
לַחֹמֶר	la-**cho**-mer	for mortar
לְכֻלָּם	l-chool-**lam**	for all of them
לָנוּ	**la**-nu	for us/ourselves
לַעֲשׂוֹת	la-a-**sot**	to make/do
לִרְאֹת	lir-**ot**	to see

מ

מֵהֶם	may-**hem**	from them
מִקֶּדֶם	meek-**ke**-dem	from the east
מִשָּׁם	meesh-**sham**	from there

נ

נִבְנֶה	neev-**ne**	we will build
נִלְבְּנָה לְבֵנִים	neel-b-**na** l-vay-**neem**	we will make bricks
נָפוּץ	na-**foots**	be scattered
נֵרְדָה	nay-r-**da**	let us go down

ע

עִיר	**eer**	city
עַל	**al**	on
עַל כֵּן	al **kayn**	therefore
עַל פְּנֵי	al p-**nay**	on the face of
עַם	**am**	people

פ

פֶּן	**pen**	lest
פְּנֵי	p-**nay**	the face of

ק

קָרָא	ka-**ra**	he called/it was called

ר

רֵעֵהוּ	ray-**ay**-hoo	friend

שֵׁם	**shaym**	name
שָׁם	**sham**	there
שְׁמָהּ	sh-**ma**	its name
שִׁנְעָר	sheen-**ar**	Shinar

שָׂפָה	sa-**fa**	language
שְׂפַת	s-**fat**	language of
שְׂפָתָם	s-fa-**tam**	their language